Nostalgia Itches like a Bug Bite

Nostalgia Itches like a Bug Bite

Pileigh Anoush Shahinian

LIGHTNING TOWER PRESS

Nostalgia Itches like a Bug Bite by Pileigh Anoush Shahinian

Published by Lightning Tower Press, LLC
P.O. Box 381
Shoreham, NY 11786

Copyright © 2024 Pileigh Anoush Shahinian

Library of Congress Control Number: 2024948619

All rights reserved. No portion of this book may be reproduced in any form without permission from the publisher, except as permitted by U.S. copyright law. For permissions, address Lightning Tower Press, LLC.
lightningtowerpress@gmail.com

Cover design by Pileigh Anoush Shahinian

ISBN 979-8-9865558-3-6 (Print)
ISBN 979-8-9865558-4-3 (Ebook)

Printed in the United States.

First Edition: 2025

10 9 8 7 6 5 4 3

To those who lie awake dreaming of yesteryears, who scratch mosquito bites until they bleed, and feel a twinge of nostalgia around every corner.

Table of Contents

I. Insectile Introspection   1

Insectile Introspection   3

II. A Multitude of Meanings   9

Mosquito	11
Lacewing	13
Earthworm	15
Firefly	17
Dragonfly	19
Cicada	21
Bee	23
Moth	25
Ladybug	27
Cricket	29
Spider	31
Silverfish	33
Grasshopper	35
Gnat	37
Tick	39
Pillbug	41
Inchworm	43
Fly	45
Ant	47
Praying Mantis	49

Flea *an interlude*	51
Termite	53
Yellowjacket	55
Locust	57
Cockroach	59
Millipede	61
Stick Bug	63
Caddisfly	65
Concrete Mite	67
Bedbug	69
Beetle	71
Stick Bug	73
Booklouse	75
Leaf Bug	77
Wasp	79
Lice	81
Centipede	83
Earwig	85
Water Strider *a lullaby*	87
Mayfly	89
Caterpillar to Butterfly: Metamorphosis	91

Acknowledgements   93

About the Author   95

Part One:
Insectile Introspection

Insectile Introspection

Itchy arms from mosquito bites—
"I told you to put that bug spray on!"
But there's so much to do on summer nights,
Without enough time to reflect upon.

I can't help but see a deeper meaning
In even the most straightforward and mundane.
Like the pattern belonging to a lacewing,
Her wings' implications flood my brain.

The insects' presence helps explain
Many a random little thing—
Like earthworms every time there's rain,
Relishing in the relief it'll bring.

Under dusk and cloud-like wisps,
Chasing fireflies at twilight.
They crawl along my fingertips—
When they blink I feel delight.

I squint my eyes and shake my head
To trail a metallic dragonfly.
Instead of a pause, she zooms by instead—
As if she, too, knows how fast time goes by.

Cicada symphonies signal in
A season's start or end.
Their song doesn't quite conclude or begin—
It simply is as their voices blend.

A honeybee drunk with pollen
Buzzes happily through the air.
His countenance becomes crestfallen—
Reminded of the stinger he must bear.

4 | | Nostalgia Itches like a Bug Bite

The moths watch as children play
With butterflies in the sun.
Yet, when they also dare to stay,
Kids scream and start to run.

Watching as the bug called lady
Moves in circles on my palm.
I count her spots where it's shady—
The symmetry keeps me calm.

The cricket chirps are lullabies.
The troubles of the day forgiven.
Their unified voice fills the skies—
Tucked safely into bed, I listen.

I swat away a spider's web,
Shaking silk from my two hands.
Guilty tears flow and ebb—
Such an intricate home no longer stands.

The silverfish scurry away from light,
Like someone not wanting to be found.
The absence of light still gives me a fright
To this day by how it keeps us bound.

The grasshopper leaps from blade to blade
Named for its very intent.
Would I ever call a spade for a spade,
And if so, to what extent?

If you tilt your head to the side and gaze
In the distance just like that,
You might just see a swarming haze—
All starting from a single gnat.

Keep an eye out for ticks;
They hide in the tallest grass.

They'll latch onto anything that sticks—
Do they know of the disease they'll pass?

The pillbug curls inside its skin—
A roly poly under anywhere wet.
Never to let anything in,
Hiding, but unable to forget.

A giggle escapes my lips
As the inch worm makes his way.
He scrunches his body in little dips—
One inch at a time, one would say.

The fly on the wall may fantasize
All that they observe.
Their compound eyes can memorize
What they think that they deserve.

The ants go marching one by one.
I wonder what keeps them going—
I think about how much work they've done,
And the colony they're growing.

With hands pressed, the praying mantis
Is remarkably pious and devout.
They're most known for their stillness—
A rare example of living without doubt.

The poems inside my head
Are itching to come out,
Like fleas on the back of a purebred:
When they bite, I have to shout.

A log filled with holes along your path
Cracks beneath your feet.
When the weight of words enables wrath,
The termites' feast is complete.

We don't tend to see that the things we despise
Share characteristics with us;
Like the yellowjacket before our very eyes,
Stings the same way we put up a fuss.

Go the extra mile
To make sure it all will last.
It may only be a little while,
Until the locusts return fast.

Open up your heart and mind,
Let hope in and just maybe,
 You will learn to love and be as kind
As a mother cockroach who holds her baby.

Thirteen thousand species of
The little millipede,
Hiding from the world above–
Making neighbors with a seed.

"Did that twig just move?"
You ask with a sudden start.
He sprawls out in order to prove,
That the stick bug has a beating heart.

Drawn to the light like a caddisfly–
Its warmth is so appealing.
Be careful of how hard you try;
The thing you love can be your undoing.

The stain that the concrete mite left behind
Reflects his very essence.
His inner and outer appearance aligned:
A legacy that prevents obsolescence.

With the covers under my chin,
Not a single fear in sight,

Until the last thing I hear as I settle in:
"Sleep tight, don't let the bedbugs bite!"

Once honored by civilizations of old,
The beetle has lost its significance.
Who used to guide rulers to the afterlife foretold,
Today is the opposite of magnificence.

The stink bug's odor gave him his name:
He is hated and mocked by all.
Yet he undeservedly takes the blame
For protecting himself from the fall.

Get lost inside a story,
Make a novel your home.
Like a booklouse in its glory,
Through chapters you will roam.

Shrinking from the spotlight,
In comfortable camouflage.
Leaf bugs hide in plain sight–
Perception's subtle sabotage.

Acting out of self defense,
Once bitten twice shy.
Fooled by poison's sweet pretense,
A wasp would sting before she'd cry.

Absentmindedly scratch your head,
Fear wells up inside you.
It's lice! The thing I most dread!
It was just a little itch– phew!

I always thought that a centipede's legs
Would add up to one hundred even.
Beneath truth's cup lies assumption's dregs:
It was only something to believe in.

Nostalgia Itches like a Bug Bite

If you're confident in who you are,
The earwigs don't stand a chance.
Inside your brain they won't get very far—
If you hold fast to your will and your stance.

As you nod off to sleep, think about this:
How the water strider's stroll upon the pond
Is daring yet easy, courageous and bliss,
Like your dreams as you journey beyond.

The mayflies do not live very long,
But every summer they come back.
Life is short, but memories are strong
Of growing up on the cul-de-sac.

Am I the butterfly fresh from the cocoon?
Or maybe I'm still in my shell.
Not knowing is alright, because one day soon—
Everyone will be able to tell.

Part Two:
A Multitude of Meanings

Itchy arms from mosquito bites—
"I told you to put that bug spray on!"
But there's so much to do on summer nights,
Without enough time to reflect upon.

Mosquito

That feeling—
That keeps you up at night,
That when you least expect it
A memory.
A song.
A game.
A smell.
Starts to itch and itch and itch
Until it nags at your heart
And you're there.
You're right there where you were,
And it nags.
And it itches.
But in the best way,
And it feels oh so good
When you scratch it,
Because it's familiar—
And it only stings because it's gone.

*I can't help but see a deeper meaning
In even the most straightforward and mundane.
Like the pattern belonging to a lacewing,
Her wings' implications flood my brain.*

Lacewing

I am cursed with creativity,
Burdened with the nagging notion
That not everything is as it seems.
I cannot look at a lacewing
And simply see an insect.
I have no choice
But to *analyze* its structure
And *memorize* the pattern and
Intricate design of its wings.
I cannot take anything at surface level:
There is always something
Deeper.

*The insects' presence helps explain
Many a random little thing—
Like earthworms every time there's rain,
Relishing in the relief it'll bring.*

Earthworm

The worms in the dirt
Pay no mind
To the way we run away from
The rain.
They come to the surface
To experience the droplets
On their strange slimey bodies,
And we squeal in disgust
When we see them—
While all they do is *exist*.

Under dusk and cloud-like wisps,
Chasing fireflies at twilight.
They crawl along my fingertips–
When they blink I feel delight.

Firefly

Look out the window–
The evening air is just right.
The receding light
Is enough–
Not *not* quite nighttime.
There's a sparkle of lights
Dancing near the trees.
If you hurry you'll catch one.
Be patient.
When you see the flash again,
Reach for it
And get dizzy trying to keep track
Of the pattern they're following.
It's hard to tell
Where they go when
They're not shining–
But, because they can,
They'll shine again
So bright you can't miss it.
And when you see it
You can
Gently
Capture it between your hands
And feel their tiny feet
Walk around
And watch the space light up–
In the gaps between your fingers
When they dare to glow.

I squint my eyes and shake my head
To trail a metallic dragonfly.
Instead of a pause, she zooms by instead–
As if she, too, knows how fast time goes by.

Dragonfly

The dragonfly hovers in midair—
For only a moment
Before zooming by.
Her spirit reflects her namesake,
She is brilliant
And radiant
And she gleams with the
Scales of a dragon.
Her delicate wings
Pound and pound
To carry her from place to place.
If she stops and looks around,
She may not recognize
Where she has ended up.
So, she'd rather keep flying—
Because at least she knows
That she does that well.

Cicada symphonies signal in
A season's start or end.
Their song doesn't quite conclude or begin–
It simply is as their voices blend.

Cicada

As cicada symphonies
Signal a new season,
We grumble and complain
That their song is distorted.
As if they can choose
What sound they make–
They work with
What they've been given.

*A honeybee drunk with pollen
Buzzes happily through the air.
His countenance becomes crestfallen–
Reminded of the stinger he must bear.*

Bee

The busiest of worker bees
Spends their nine to five
Making something sweet,
While the danger of their sting
Looms overhead.
What finality is attached
To an act of violence—
Stinging another
Brings about *the end of self*.
But for now,
Let's think about *honey*.
And how they have a queen,
And how they create a colony,
In the most unconventional of spaces—
With a hexagon pattern, no less,
And are striped with black and yellow.

The moths watch as children play
With butterflies in the sun.
Yet, when they also dare to stay,
Kids scream and start to run.

Moth

She resembles a butterfly,
But not enough
To be as conventionally beautiful.
A butterfly is known as a symbol of grace,
While a moth is feared for her broad frame
And the fuzz that covers her body.
Do they not both possess a desirable pattern across their wings?
Do they not both soar through the air?
Perhaps she tears through the fabric
Of humanity's clothes
In revenge
For what they have painted her to be:
"If they can't see my garments as beautiful, I will destroy theirs."

Watching as the bug called lady
Moves in circles on my palm.
I count her spots where it's shady–
The symmetry keeps me calm.

Ladybug

I don't believe in luck.
I believe that
All the delightful things
We experience
Are designed.
The way I'm loved
Is not a coincidence,
A stroke of happenstance.
It would be
Belittling
To amount it as such.
My life has purpose–
It has highs and lows.
But not for a second do I think
It's all simply an accident,
Just like a ladybug's spots.

The cricket chirps are lullabies.
The troubles of the day forgiven.
Their unified voice fills the skies—
Tucked safely into bed, I listen.

Cricket

When the skies are alive
With the crickets' chirps,
Society plugs its ears.
But they rub and rub
And rub and rub
Their little legs together,
And sing their song
As loud as they can.
Because that's what they do.
And rather than be lured
To sleep by their lullaby,
We complain and wonder
"When will it end?"
Maybe we should ask
"How did it start?"
"And why?"

*I swat away a spider's web,
Shaking silk from my two hands.
Guilty tears flow and ebb –
Such an intricate home no longer stands.*

Spider

A spider's home is strong yet fragile—
Beautiful but nearly invisible,
Deadly yet inviting.
So when her work
Is blown to the wind
Or dismantled by human hands,
Does she not mourn?
Does she not regret *giving of her body*
To make this home?
Or does she move on,
And begin anew—
Strand by strand?

The silverfish scurry away from light,
Like someone not wanting to be found.
The absence of light still gives me a fright
To this day by how it keeps us bound.

Silverfish

I am still afraid of the dark.
Rather,
I am afraid of *what I cannot see* in the dark.
I dislike not seeing;
I hate the feeling of not knowing
What may be right in front of me.
As a child, I would frantically
Open and close my eyes in the dark,
Alarmed by how there was no difference
Due to the absence of light.
Even now, the worst behavior is always
Concealed by darkness.
Just like how the silverfish scurry away from the light,
So is the shroud of night a hiding place
For those who do not want to be caught.

The grasshopper leaps from blade to blade
Named for its very intent.
Would I ever call a spade for a spade,
And if so, to what extent?

Grasshopper

What is this envy?
Oh, to be a small green bug
Who hops in the grass,
Simply because
His name is grasshopper.
The simplicity of his purpose
Is *irritating*.
Why are we so much more
Complicated?
Would it be horrible to be named
After the things we would set out to do?
At least we would know
Exactly
What we were made for.

If you tilt your head to the side and gaze
In the distance just like that,
You might just see a swarming haze–
All starting from a single gnat.

Gnat

You sort of can't quite see them,
Unless you look from just the right angle.
But as soon as you notice them,
They're impossible to ignore.
You can wave your hand as you walk by–
You can wave away that
Deep
Deep
Thought,
But just like how the gnats swarm,
One bad thought always leads to another.

Keep an eye out for ticks;
They hide in the tallest grass.
They'll latch onto anything that sticks–
Do they know of the disease they'll pass?

Tick

Check yourself for ticks before
Coming back inside the house.
Tick rhymes with trick,
So be careful–
They blend right into
Birthmarks and scabs.
They sneak into your skin,
Fill you with fear:
Bullseye colored rash.
But you have to admire their resilience, right?
They won't go down without a fight.
One must wonder if they know
The harm that they can cause us,
Or if they're simply looking
For a place to make their own.

The pillbug curls inside its skin—
A roly poly under anywhere wet.
Never to let anything in,
Hiding, but unable to forget.

Pillbug

My body is my armor.
When I'm hurt,
I can turn inside myself
Without letting it show.
I can feel my emotions
So *tangibly*
It's as if they're in my skin.
So, when it's time,
I can hide behind
Humor.
Happiness.
But aren't I an open book?
Aren't I just a little roly poly bug,
Looking for someplace damp?

A giggle escapes my lips
As the inch worm makes his way.
He scrunches his body in little dips—
One inch at a time, one would say.

Inch Worm

The inch worm folds himself in half
To move forward
Every move he makes
Brings his new end to his old beginning
He catches up to himself in every inch
He is small,
But he is mighty.
Named for his length,
Classified by his determination
To continue moving
Inch
By
Inch.

The fly on the wall may fantasize
All that they observe.
Their compound eyes can memorize
What they think that they deserve.

F*ly*

A fly on the wall.
Never in the room, fully,
Just an *observer*.
But still,
With those compound eyes,
They can pretend they are a part of it–
A part of everything.
Seeing all that is reflected back at them
A thousand times over.
Every intricate detail,
Every laugh.
Every nuance.
It's so lovely,
You can almost forget
It isn't real.
You can almost ignore
The swatter positioned towards you.

The ants go marching one by one.
I wonder what keeps them going—
I think about how much work they've done,
And the colony they're growing.

Ant

The tiniest of the
Animal kingdom
Do not know how truly
Powerful they are.
United in one body,
They become a formidable threat.
For Rome was not built in a day,
And we praise the craftsmanship
Of society and civilization–
Is the colony of an ant insignificant?
How different are they really?
They carry more than they can manage,
They follow a leader,
They all look the same,
They form families,
And homes.
And towns.
And cities.
And we tear down their walls
Without a second glance
Simply because
They were born under our feet.

With hands pressed, the praying mantis
Is remarkably pious and devout.
They're most known for their stillness—
A rare example of living without doubt.

Praying Mantis

Hands wrung in prayer
For so long
Eventually take the shape
Of those of a praying mantis.
Made with a physical connection
To the spiritual—
Created to praise.
The muscle memory:
Head bowed.
Heart raised.
Hands folded.
A mantis-like faith
Innate.
Intuitive.
Instinctual.

The poems inside my head
Are itching to come out,
Like fleas on the back of a purebred:
When they bite, I have to shout.

Flea *an interlude*

The flea infestation is well underway.
They've mistaken my head for the back of a dog:
Digging and *biting* and *urging* me on.
When I sit down to write,
They are silent and unmoving.
Yet in my unguarded moments,
They *sink their teeth* into my mind,
Forcing me to stop dead in my tracks
And pick up my pen
To frantically record
The poem that is *itching to get out*.

A log filled with holes along your path
Cracks beneath your feet.
When the weight of words enables wrath,
The termites' feast is complete.

Termite

It always starts so simply:
You thought you were amusing,
Calling me names,
Impressing your friends.
You were the termite
Who burrowed into wood.
Your words created *holes in my skin.*
You can try to apologize,
You can try to fill the gaps,
But the more you take away,
The bigger it gets.
And while it may look like I'm intact,
The minute you stepped on me
I crumbled.

We don't tend to see that the things we despise
Share characteristics with us;
Like the yellowjacket before our very eyes,
Stings the same way we put up a fuss.

Yellowjacket

We, the people, hate them.
Yet we share many qualities:
We are usually non-aggressive *(one would hope)*
Unless *provoked*.
We don our uniforms for work,
Our favorite *yellow jackets*,
And we do what we are asked to do.
We put our leaders on pedestals,
And we defend them like no one's business.
We build our homes well,
And protect them even better.
And if someone gets too close,
They'll get stung
Repeatedly.

*Go the extra mile
To make sure it all will last.
It may only be a little while,
Until the locusts return fast.*

Locust

Protecting your *peace* is a *process*.
You can't ignore the signs
And then expect nothing to fail.
You must *proactively picture*
What might just happen.
Live and *learn*, as they say:
Don't leave room for the chance that
Your labor will be in vain.
When the locusts come to eat your crops,
Maybe this time you'll stop them:
Await and *anticipate*.
Prevent and *prepare*.

*Open up your heart and mind,
Let hope in and just maybe,
You will learn to love and be as kind
As a mother cockroach who holds her baby.*

Cockroach

Find joy in the simple,
Find happiness in the bland,
Find love in the spiteful,
Find hope in the darkest of places.
If you keep an open mind and heart,
Both will be filled to the brim.
After all,
Even a mother cockroach
Holds her baby tight
And thinks he is the most beautiful thing.

*Thirteen thousand species of
The little millipede,
Hiding from the world above—
Making neighbors with a seed.*

Millipede

Maybe I'll dig a little deeper,
If I keep looking down,
Maybe things will
Start to look up.
Like a millipede who burrows
Down
Down
Down
Into the earth.
Until *everything* I see
Is *nothing,*
And the *nothing* that I see
Is *everything.*
Deconstructing.
Decomposing.

"Did that twig just move?"
You ask with a sudden start.
He sprawls out in order to prove,
That the stick bug has a beating heart.

Stick Bug

He sees himself wherever he goes.
Disguised and protected,
The stick bug is a marvel.
Does he wonder what lies before him?
Could it be a brother, a friend—
Or just another inanimate plant
That he inevitably looks like?
He ponders how other insects are distinct,
Set apart from the world they reside in.
They can dare to be *different;*
They can dare to *dream,*
But the stick bug must, well, stick
To his resemblance to home
His fate has been determined
Forced conformity.

*Drawn to the light like a caddisfly—
Its warmth is so appealing.
Be careful of how hard you try;
The thing you love can be your undoing.*

Caddisfly

I'm in love with the lantern,
Or the lamp,
Or the fluorescent light strip—
Whichever can provide me with as much light as possible
As quickly as possible.
I am intoxicated
By the warmth and the glow and the shine
That light brings.
Illumination is everything:
Refreshing, renewing, reinvigorating.
They say that distance makes the heart grow fonder,
And my attraction becomes hunger
At the thought of being one with the sun—
Something strange happens
Whenever I dare to approach.
I am struck by a sudden heat,
An overwhelming burning sensation,
That consumes my entire body:
That's how I know it's love.
Every caddisfly I've ever known
Has shared in my object of affection,
But I will be the first to meet her.
I brace myself for flight:
I embark.
I am almost there,
I am nearly there,
I could burst with excitement!
My vision blurs as we collide and I open my mouth to—
...

The stain that the concrete mite left behind
Reflects his very essence.
His inner and outer appearance aligned:
A legacy that prevents obsolescence.

Concrete Mite

Looks can be deceiving;
This is undeniably true.
And yet, oftentimes they aren't—
Sometimes what you see *is* what you get.
You can admire a book by its cover
Only to find that its contents are equally as loveable.
The spot left behind by a concrete mite
On the curb where he lost his life,
Is exactly what you would expect it to be:
A single scarlet spot on a concrete canvas.
So maybe, just maybe,
The things that are inside of us
Are the things we leave behind.

With the covers under my chin,
Not a single fear in sight,
Until the last thing I hear as I settle in:
"Sleep tight, don't let the bedbugs bite!"

Bedbug

I may or may not have had
An irrational fear
Of bed bugs.
I was always told
To not let them bite,
But how would I stop them?
If they made up their minds
To bite me,
What would I do?
Yet, in all my years,
I have never encountered
A single bed bug.
In fact, I can't even think
Of one person I know who has had them
(To my knowledge, that is).
Funny how repeated warnings
Can speak fears into existence.

Once honored by civilizations of old,
The beetle has lost its significance.
Who used to guide rulers to the afterlife foretold,
Today is the opposite of magnificence.

Beetle

The ancient Egyptians,
Without any of the technology we take for granted today,
Carved little scarabs out of precious metals
And placed them over the hearts
Of fallen pharaohs,
In hopes that the little beetle
Would ensure that their ruler
Had a chance of surviving the afterlife.
And now when we see such a bug,
We crush it just because we can.

*The stink bug's odor gave him his name:
He is hated and mocked by all.
Yet he undeservedly takes the blame
For protecting himself from the fall.*

Stink Bug

Named for the odor he produces,
The stink bug's reputation precedes him.
The object of ridicule:
When he is spotted, he is mocked.
Yet we never dwell upon why
He is the way that he is.
Did you know that he acts out of fear?
To protect himself, to preserve his life?
Self defense can make anyone desperate.

Get lost inside a story,
Make a novel your home.
Like a booklouse in its glory,
Through chapters you will roam.

Booklouse

I want to be a booklouse.
Yes, you read that line correctly.
I want to dive so deeply
That I imbed my very body
Into the binding of a novel,
I want to tattoo the words along my skin,
And inhale the pages
Until I memorize passages
And make each chapter
A place to rest my head.

*Shrinking from the spotlight,
In comfortable camouflage.
Leaf bugs hide in plain sight—
Perception's subtle sabotage.*

Leaf Bug

Maybe if I angle myself
Against this leaf
In such a way,
No one will notice me.
If I hold my breath and wait,
They will pass me by.
As long as they don't look hard enough,
If I model myself
After what surrounds me,
I will fade into the background.
I will avoid inspection.
I will escape perception.

Acting out of self defense,
Once bitten twice shy.
Fooled by poison's sweet pretense,
A wasp would sting before she'd cry.

Wasp

Lure me in with your sugared words,
As lies drip from your mouth.
My *brain* recognizes the taste as *bitter*,
But my *heart* sees only *sweetness*.
Maybe that's why I'm sharp and biting:
A villain born from my hero–
A wasp in a field of flowers.

Absentmindedly scratch your head,
Fear wells up inside you.
It's lice! The thing I most dread!
It was just a little itch— phew!

Lice

They make your head their home,
They burrow inside your follicles,
They nest within your strands.
It's contagious, they say,
Usually caught at school.
All it takes is one to start it all:
Everyone loves being a follower.
You think you can handle it–
It's just a little itch,
Until they're all *on* your head
Until they're all *in* your head
And suddenly that one itch
Becomes unbelievably unbearable.
You buy the special comb,
You use the special shampoo,
And everyone laughs at you and
Makes you cut your hair–
Wait
Are we still talking about lice?

*I always thought that a centipede's legs
Would add up to one hundred even.
Beneath truth's cup lies assumption's dregs:
It was only something to believe in.*

Centipede

I like to be careful,
I like to be *right*.
I'd count every little leg on a centipede
Just to make sure
There's one hundred.
I'd watch it wriggle beneath my fingers
As I double and triple check,
Only to discover
That a perfect one hundred
Is a *myth*.
They can have many more or much less.
The realization is *jarring*,
So maybe I shouldn't get too close
On second thought,
Because then I'd realize
Their very name is *deception*.

If you're confident in who you are,
The earwigs don't stand a chance.
Inside your brain they won't get very far —
If you hold fast to your will and your stance.

Earwig

Be strong in who you are!
Be unabashedly you!
So that when the earwigs creep in your head,
They won't whisper wicked words
That eat away at your brain.
Instead, you can shake them loose
And send them tumbling out of your thoughts,
So that you can laugh through the lies
And be free!

As you nod off to sleep, think about this:
How the water strider's stroll upon the pond
Is daring yet easy, courageous and bliss,
Like your dreams as you journey beyond.

Water Strider *a lullaby*

As your eyelids are heavy laden with sleep,
Dance upon the surface of the pond
Like a little water strider.
Float away from your fears
As you feel entirely weightless.
Glide towards your endless dreams;
Do a summersault over the moon.
Blow a kiss at a shooting star,
And as the sun lays her head
On the rolling pillow plains,
Snuggle up beside her,
And allow her warmth to surround you
To keep you safe tonight and always.

*The mayflies do not live very long,
But every summer they come back.
Life is short, but memories are strong
Of growing up on the cul-de-sac.*

Mayfly

Let's live like we're young in the summertime—
Because we are.
In fact, we will never be this young again:
A statement whose truth rings even more true every second.
Let's not think about
What has to be done in the fall,
Or the ever present feeling of
Time
Slipping
Away.
Even though the mayfly is known for its short lifespan,
It is also known for its emergence during summer months.
Thus,
Let *us* be mayflies.
Let us soar above the fears and the doubts,
Let us gather together,
And ride our bikes around the loop of the cul-de-sac
Until we are right back where we started.

Am I the butterfly fresh from the cocoon?
Or maybe I'm still in my shell.
Not knowing is alright, because one day soon—
Everyone will be able to tell.

Caterpillar to Butterfly: Metamorphosis

Everyone keeps telling me
To change,
To grow,
To move on
And move out,
But I like my cocoon.
Sure, sometimes
It's too small,
And sometimes
It gets dark,
But other times
The sun shines
Just perfectly enough
And I am surrounded
By a *warmth*
That brings me back
To the days of being
A caterpillar.
And I'm scared to break free
Because I've heard that butterflies *bleed* when they're *reborn*.
What if I don't know how
To be a butterfly?
What if the other butterflies soar
And I'll only fall?
What if I am
Unrecognizable?
Will I forget how lovely it was
To be a caterpillar?
Something inside me

Craves to know
What the intricate pattern
On my wings will look like,
How the fresh breeze
Will feel on my face
As I leave the leaves behind.
But–
What's the rush?
I'll be a butterfly for
The rest of my life,
But I'll never be a caterpillar again.
The leaf I cling to
As I lay curled up,
Safe and huddled
From the outside world,
My cocoon
Is home.

Acknowledgements

It feels absolutely necessary to share that I wrote the final piece of this collection on a Thursday afternoon in July, wearing a pair of purple pajamas in my childhood bed. The journey that *Nostalgia Itches like a Bug Bite* has taken me on has been one of the most fulfilling in my life, and I must offer acknowledgements to those who have made it possible.

First and foremost, I must thank my Lord and Savior Jesus Christ for creating me with a nostalgic heart, and for making even the smallest of creatures so complex and fascinating. May we forever find God in the little things as often as we do in the big things.

Secondly, I must thank my family for providing me with such a wonderful childhood. It is one thing to think fondly of the past, but it is another blessing entirely to feel such remorse about having to grow up because of how wonderful your youth was. To my sister, Lucine, for being my confidant, playmate, and most importantly, truest friend. To my mom, Laurie, for always being my biggest supporter, and who always wears the title of "mom" the loudest and proudest amid her medical struggles. To my dad, Vasken, for always being there for whatever I need, whether it be an uplifting joke, a deep conversation, a word of advice, or something that combines those three. Thank you both for laying a strong foundation for Lucine and I, allowing us to embrace our girlhood freely and crazily, and for showing us how to bring up children in this world. Mom, Dad, Lucine, thank you for showering me with endless love, and for providing the inspiration for this very collection. Without you, there would be nothing to wish I could escape back to.

To my friends, who have shared in my excitement for this publication, for reading scattered poems along the way, and for accepting me at my highest and lowest points: thank you. You are all a part of this project and the feelings behind these pieces, and I love you all dearly.

Lastly, I would like to thank anyone and everyone who has read this collection. I hope that my words have spoken to you in some way. Whether these poems make you laugh or cry, or cause you to think either forwards or backwards, I invite you to just *feel*. Embrace whatever the poems invoke, and revel in the idea that words arranged on a page in such a way have power to influence our emotions. Next time you get a mosquito bite, I hope you think of me.

About the Author

Pileigh Anoush Shahinian is a poet and writer from Long Island, New York. "Nostalgia Itches like a Bug Bite" is her first publication, but she has been writing for as long as she has known how to. She graduated with her bachelor's degree in English Adolescent Education with a minor in Religious Studies in May of 2024 from St. Joseph's University in Patchogue, New York. Currently, she is an online graduate student at Concordia University, pursuing her Master's degree in Creative Writing.

www.ingramcontent.com/pod-product-compliance
Lightning Source LLC
Chambersburg PA
CBHW020553030426
42337CB00013B/1083